To Jacob,

Sing it Loud!

Learn to Read!

Onward to Anything!

Aloha

[signature]

P.S. Jiu Jitsu

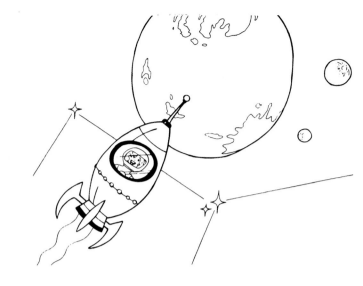

The Second Verse to the ABCs
Reading as The Power of Anything

by Ryan William Nohea Garcia

Illustrated by Justin Takaha White

Foreword by Mark Victor Hansen
co-creator of *Chicken Soup for the Soul*®

"The Second Verse to the ABCs" (song) written by Ryan William Nohea Garcia.
Copyright © 2017 Quid Promo Quo, LLC.

This song is dedicated to the Creative Commons under an Attribution-ShareAlike license (BY-SA) version 4.0.

License details available at creativecommons.org/licenses/by-sa/4.0

Please participate in and support the #SecondVerseABC Project.
Visit SecondVerseABC.com for more information. Thank you.

The Second Verse to the ABCs (book)
Copyright © 2017 Quid Promo Quo, LLC. All rights reserved.

This book may be purchased in bulk for educational, promotional, or business use. Contact the promoter at http://www.secondverseabc.com/contact

LCCN: 2017907308
ISBN: 978-0-692-89437-8
First Edition-2017

The Second Verse to the ABCs is the first in a series.

Published by Quid Promo Quo, LLC. http://www.SecondVerseABC.com
Printed in a Special Economic Zone in Shenzhen, China.

Thanks to CultureShocka.com (illustrations), Noletorious.com (layout), and Luna Daisy (Luna's Handwriting font, available at fontspace.com/lunadaisy).

For Marlo, Alana, and Logan
me ke aloha pumehana

Origin and Theory of "The Second Verse to the ABCs"

Reading opens the world. As first-time parents-to-be, Marlo and I hoped our daughter would become a precocious reader. To this end I wrote "The Second Verse to the ABCs" attempting to simplify and deliver the mechanics of reading in lyrics set to a familiar melody: the "ABCs."

Our theory went if we sang "The Second Verse to the ABCs" alongside the "ABCs" and other children's songs our daughter might more easily conceptualize and learn to read—or sooner grasp the significance of letters and writing. It sure couldn't hurt, anyway.

So we sang "The Second Verse to the ABCs" to her at least as often as any other song. When she could talk she asked about letters, words, and reading, alongside animals, stars, and spiders. Her questions opened far-ranging discussions about reading and learning, and inspired the child-led Socratic dialogue in *The Second Verse to the ABCs*.

We are overjoyed our daughter became a precocious reader, and quickly. She is onward to anything!

We hope the same for our son. We think "The Second Verse to the ABCs" is worth all the "Old MacDonalds," "Twinkle Twinkles," and "Itsy Bitsy Spiders" in the world, and hope you will too.

We encourage you to sing "The Second Verse to the ABCs" with as many children as possible. Singing, teaching, sharing, and performing "The Second Verse to the ABCs" can help children learn to read—or sooner grasp the significance of letters and writing. It sure can't hurt, anyway, to deliver the mechanics of reading early and often. Singing "The Second Verse" takes less than a minute, and it's catchy!

We hope you enjoy this book and benefit from the song. Thank you for your interest and support for the #SecondVerseABC Project.

Onward to Anything!

Ryan & Marlo

Foreword by Mark Victor Hansen
co-creator of the *Chicken Soup for the Soul*® series

Reading is freedom. Reading is joy. Reading is love manifest in good thinking form. I love to read and I love to write. And I do everything I can to inspire others to do the same, or more.

My parents were illiterate Danes with minor educations. Danish was the first language spoken in our home, and we lacked books and other reading material. I had great reading difficulty, and my school sent me to remedial reading class from first through sixth grade.

It was one of the greatest gifts I could have ever been given. I went from being an inferior reader to a world-class speed reader that could absorb and have high comprehension at 4,000 words per minute. Blessings on all those people who helped me learn to read better because I became the world's best-selling author as co-creator of the *Chicken Soup for the Soul* series, which has sold more books than anything other than the Bible—over 500 million and counting.

Recently my wife Crystal and I accepted The Power of Excellence Award from Dr. Benjamin and his wife Candy Carson, founders of the Carson Scholars Fund.

Ben's inspiring story began with an unusual level of difficulty: broken home, poverty, and a thirteen year-old mother with a third-grade education. But she was determined to see her sons succeed.

When Ben was in third grade she said "You are no longer going to fail out of school. You and your brother are going to the public library and getting two books to read per week." So Ben and his brother got books, read them, and wrote book reports about them. Their mother checked, underlined, and highlighted their reports. They read and read and read. The Carson boys never discovered their mother could scarcely read. From third to fourth grade Ben went from the bottom to the top of the class. Ben did so well that he attended Yale medical school, became a neurosurgeon at John Hopkins, and performed over 15,000 pediatric neurosurgeries—all because of his love of reading.

These achievements would be good enough alone, but in 1994 Dr. Carson and his wife started the Carson Scholars Fund, which awards over 500 $1,000 scholarships annually to high achieving students who contribute to their communities.

To date the Carson Scholars Fund has awarded over 7,300 scholarships totaling $4.7 million. The Ben Carson Reading Project, an initiative of the Carson Scholars Fund, has created over 160 reading rooms in twenty-two states, providing a literacy enriched environment in schools where children can discover the joy of independent leisure reading and develop high-level reading skills unlocking their full potential.

This is highly important work: athletics and entertainment should not be the only things hallowed in every elementary, junior high, and high school. We ought to respect those with a good education and humanitarian ethics.

The next challenge the Carson Scholars Fund is addressing is, like my childhood home, many children's homes and community libraries lack books and reading material. Crystal and I are committed to helping The Carson Scholars Fund place more books in children's hands. I've told Ben that I will talk to every author and publisher I know about contributing books and electronic books. Let's get everyone to fall in love with reading and advancing knowledge because America and the world needs to be better read. Crystal and I are dedicated to this cause.

We love this book—*The Second Verse to the ABCs*—because it teaches and inspires children to start reading at a young age and make a difference. This is the beginning of a life of liberated freedom, knowledge, information, and most importantly good judgement and the discernment called wisdom.

We are participating in the #SecondVerseABC Project and encourage everyone to join us. Sing, teach, and perform "The Second Verse to the ABCs" and share your Anything. Our Anything—what Crystal and I work to bring about—is global energy self-sufficiency and independence from fossil fuels. When there is more than sufficient clean energy we can create plenty of fresh, potable water. With ample water we can grow abundant and nourishing food for Earth's expanding population. Onward to Anything!

Mark Victor Hansen
co-creator of the Chicken Soup for the Soul® series
co-founder & chairman of Metamorphosis Energy, LLC

What is reading, Daddy?

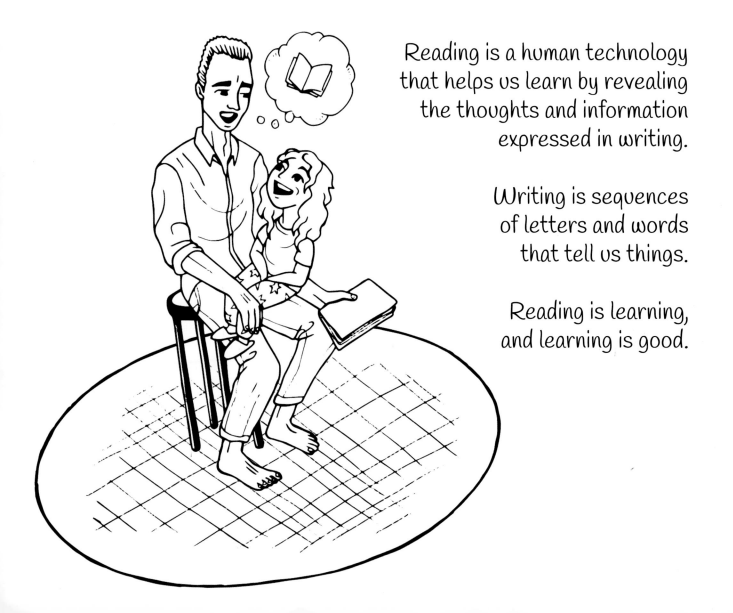

Reading is a human technology that helps us learn by revealing the thoughts and information expressed in writing.

Writing is sequences of letters and words that tell us things.

Reading is learning, and learning is good.

Why do you read, Daddy?

Because there is so much to learn!

Learning makes me smarter.

Readers can learn anything they want or need to know.

If you can read you can learn anything.

If you can learn anything you can do anything.

Reading is the Power of Anything.

Anything I want?

Yes! Anything you want, Dear One.

There are so many books
and so much digital media to read.

Readers can access thousands of
years of experience, knowledge,
and information on any subject
you can think of.

Could I read about dinosaurs?
What about birds?

Yes to both, Dear One.

And you'll be surprised at what
dinosaurs and birds have in common.
You can read and learn
anything thing you want.

Daddy, will you help me learn to read?

Yes, of course—with joy.

I will be so happy
when you can read.

Almost nothing
is more important
to me than you
learning to read,
Dear One.

Why do you so value me learning to read, Daddy?

Because the world opens to readers.

When you can learn by reading you can:

ACHIEVE anything,

BECOME anything,

and DISCOVER anything.

Readers wield the Power of Anything.

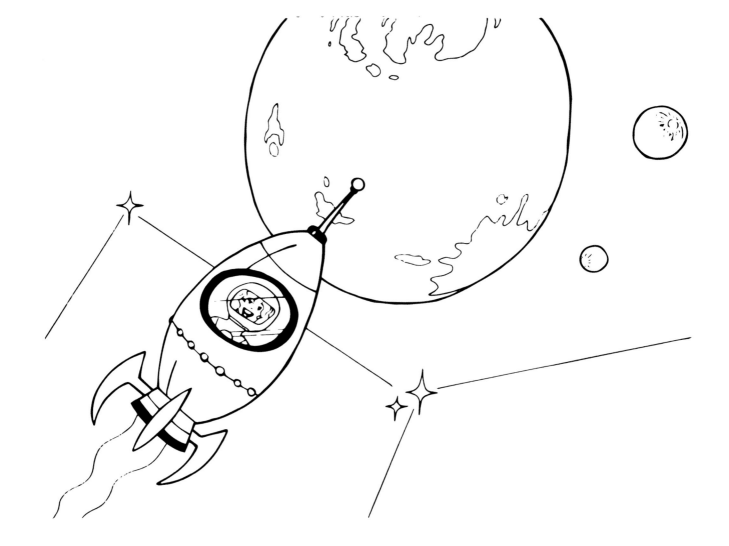

Yes! Anything you want.

Daddy, how do I read?

You read by sounding-out words:
one by one, left to right, in order.

All you have to learn is
how the letters' sounds form words.

Then, you can read any word by
sounding it out, syllable by syl-la-ble.

And that is reading, Dear One.

Can you help me remember how to read, Daddy?

Yes, of course—with joy, Dear One.

You and I will sing
"The Second Verse to the ABCs"
every day until you've memorized it.

Knowing "The Second Verse to the ABCs" will help you understand and remember how to read, just like the "ABCs" help you remember the letters.

Sing it to remember how to read.

Sing it to help others learn to read.

Be proud that you are learning to read.

Dear One, will you sing
"The Second Verse to the ABCs"
with me now?

Yes, Daddy.

So I can learn to read.

"The Second Verse to the ABCs"
sung to the melody of the ABCs

```
C                   F           C
Letters have sounds, Sounds form words

F        C         G7            C
Words form sentences, Which express thought

C            F    C           G7
All you have to do is, Learn how the letter sounds

C  F      C             G7
Fit --- together, and formulate words,

C                         F          C
Next learn their meaning, Onward to Anything!

F        C            G7        C
Sound it out, Word by word, Is reading to me
```

See The Original at SecondVerseABC.com

What's your anything
to achieve, become, or discover?

Learn, Share, Connect
www.SecondVerseABC.com
#SecondVerseABC tag your videos and posts
@SecondVerseABC fb, ig, twitter, twitch, patreon

Participate in the #SecondVerseABC Project
visit SecondVerseABC.com/project for more information.

Let's build a global learning community
join Onward to Anything—the #SecondVerseABC podcast
student and subject matter expert participation requested
visit SecondVerseABC.com/podcast for more information

#SecondVerseABC @SecondVerseABC
www.SecondVerseABC.com #OnwardtoAnything

Afterword by Michael Strong

I hope you enjoyed *The Second Verse to the ABCs*. Socratic dialogue, the question and answer format of the book, helps children develop cognitive, verbal, and interpersonal skills, and become powerful, self-aware thinkers with a firm sense of independent judgment. It will also help you understand your child's particular aptitudes, dispositions, and interests. All that is required is willingness to engage your child in spontaneous, natural learning experiences about the world around them.

I have been helping Marlo and Ryan's daughter Alana (Dear One), explore the world through Socratic dialogue via video-chats. In a recent exchange Alana and I conversed about how she could tell the difference between a bird, a flying insect, and an airplane. She clearly knew the difference—insects are not airplanes—but it required thought for her to slow down and articulate exactly how she knows that a particular flying object is, or is not, a bird. Conversations like these help develop her cognitive abilities, and she gains confidence from talking and interacting with adults about abstract thoughts.

You can incorporate Socratic Dialogue into your child's education by regularly engaging him or her in questions and answers about Anything: things to achieve, become, and discover (or anything else). Doing so helps with reading and learning, and leads to your child transitioning into reading in a fun, collaborative, social manner. Direct parental engagement with children about Anything helps lead to amazing, happy, brilliant children.

I encourage you to participate in the #SecondVerseABC Project and seek more information about how you can provide your children with a superb, personalized education at home by means of direct, loving engagement with your children. Sing, read, and discuss! Onward to Anything!

Michael Strong
educator, author, entrepreneur, and
co-founder of multiple high-performing schools
https://www.linkedin.com/in/michaelstrong1/